T0287306

The Consciousness of Place

The

Consciousness

Kashef
Chowdhury

of

Place

QUART

Whatever our invention or intervention, our engagements with *place* hardly ever end in concord. Only if we were to slow down and listen into its deep silence, could we hear of the memories and wishes of a place.

Impressions

Talk delivered at the triennial Commonwealth Association of Architects
Conference in Dhaka, in February 2013 and previously published in the
Architectural Review special issue on Kashef Chowdhury/URBANA,
December 2013.

That feeling of being in the delta: hot, humid, breezy, mosquitoes. Patches of green in a sea of greens. Look up and see an ocean in clouds. Grey, white or the colours of the sun.

Sun. That beautiful light I remember from my childhood – slashes of afternoon on the golden of the straw. I remember the smell. I remember the sounds of the straw.

When I said I love the rain, the sun and everything in between, I meant I wanted to build to enjoy the rain, the sun and everything in between. And where else but here, the home of the Brahmaputra and the Jamuna, wedded together in the softest soil, moist as the womb of the mother.

Before the shadow of the rock the Himalayas, the largest delta in the world, touches the waters of the Bay. This is Bengal, a geo-cultural region woven out of an intricate network of rivers and canals and to which all art forms respond – from the emotionally rendered Bhawaiya songs and the colours of the stitches of Nakshi-Kantha textiles, to the living and lost architecture of the delta.

Much of my childhood was spent by the side of the River Padma, which draws its waters from the Ganges. It is difficult to bring to words my memories with those waters, of the clouds – both above and soaked in reflection. And the finest and softest of all soils: the alluvial layers where the ground was still moist from receding waters. But it is not merely the impact of those elements. For me, a river is not the same again; or rain; or the darkness before a storm in monsoon. I have been forever changed by the spirituality of that land.

The tropical light introduces us to the landscape of Bengal. The strong sun's light reveals the beauty of its nature. It falls on mountains, fields of paddy and trees, but the rest is spilled light – lost light. It is the architect, who by the design of his apertures brings in this spilled light into the deep insides of his architecture. He gives it shape, lets it play or prevents it from removing his shadows. For with the darkness of shadows comes the appreciation of light, of the colour of light, of the depth of light.

Have you seen the depth of Kahn's light? At the National Assembly Building in Dhaka, Kahn brings in a silvery light, playful as the water from which the building rises. Nowhere has a space been more gracefully lit than by the magical light of *his* tropical sun.

I am in search of shadows. Shadows under a banyan tree, behind a column or from a dark cloud. Have you ever been in a forest, a temple or in a village courtyard?

Shadows have a wonderful way of celebrating the presence of light. They seem to say: we do not hide; our purpose is to reveal.

Too many times we have seen buildings naked, sunburnt, clad only in a curtain of glass. What is the purpose I say? Let us not chase the shadows away. Then we are left with a pale, dead light. Uninspiring. Unnecessary.

I return to the comfort of the shadow, which the light has brought in.

Materials? Ask me not of materials. I'm still listening to the story of the clay earth, millions of years before you have uncovered it, moulded it, burnt it. For bricks or terracotta temples. I wish to know more. And I want to learn to care. Like gold in the hands of a goldsmith. And oh! The textures, the imperfections, the feeling, the beckoning.

The building doesn't need ornament. The material *is* the ornament.

There was a time when I thought I couldn't live in the city. It was too powerful. Too much happening in too little time. Then I realised it was possible to create your own secret space in a city. It would be free from the rush elsewhere. It would have its own pace. It's own time.

Time.

Is it true that if the sun hadn't moved, there wouldn't have been time? Or is it locked in a Swiss watch or in a Japanese pendulum? I like to leave time out of my buildings. I sense that leaves out a lot of other things: styles, trends, isms and so on.

I'm tired of efficient buildings. Buildings that offer you not a moment to pause, to ponder, to wish, to recollect. Buildings that work well, better than you had wished for and give you nothing else. In an office or railway station – yes. But in a home or in front of art in an art gallery, I look for a loss of time.

Absence of time.

And then there arises the opportunity for serenity to invade. And silence. The silence of a breeze. The silence of a deep sleep. The silence of a space.

My work used to confuse me. But it was important to be confused. I sense in confusion lie the seeds of discovery, of truth. I drink a drink from the broth of seven or ten thousand, yes *thousand*, years of my history and I feel alive again. The myth, the mystery, the mysticism. The emotion, the philosophy, the chaos, the romance. Yes I'm in love with the Bengali way of life. Come away with me for an hour of the Sarod and you will know what I mean. But ask me not of my work for I create for the love of art. And ask me not of the present or of the future – I know neither.

From room to city:
Nature, culture and
other chapters

Keynote speech at the Indian Institute of Architects Convention
in Kolhapur, in May 2012.

The French have a word "immeuble", which as an adjective means immovable but as a noun, it means building. Therein lies the true nature of architecture. That is, if architecture is an art, it is an immovable art.

So unlike most other forms of art – from literature to film, from painting to music – the built architecture cannot be displayed on a wall, become part of an archive or be simply carried away. With few exceptions, architecture is forever married to the place where it is located. And to its climate, its wind, its light, its flora and fauna, and its people.

Architecture is man-made, nature is not. Nature cannot make architecture, in the same way that man cannot make nature. In his gardens, man borrows from nature or in his dams, man changes the course of nature but in reality, man cannot make nature.

Our exploration into the possibilities of architecture to be situated anywhere must begin with the complete and full understanding of the fact that architecture cannot be divorced from nature. And if such be our acceptance, then we need to devote as much energy to the study and research on nature as we do for architecture.

But this relationship between nature and architecture is, too often, less of magic and more of potent conflict. Many years ago I was reading an interview with a famous Japanese architect. He was discussing his feelings about the land before the building was constructed and he ended a chain of thoughts by saying "and the land was ready for the building". It suddenly became clear to me, at that very instant, that no land is ever ready for a building. Nature thrives on its own and never seeks nor needs the placement of any object on its land body, as it were. It is man who, for his needs, places objects in nature and on the land, and this imposition is only lessened – but never perished – by the sympathetic architect intervening most sensitively.

And yet we have examples of many older cultures showing great reverence for their land. The Aboriginal people of Australia find themselves inseparably related to the land. The spiritual link between the person and his ancestor through the land and animal species means that his link with a particular area of land cannot be taken away or transferred somewhere else. For the Aboriginal people, land is something that cannot be bought or sold – land is a source of his or her identity. To them, a new construction, even a clearing in the forest, must first be accepted by the spirit of the land and to this end they will perform elaborated rituals, one of which I myself have attended.

A similar if not more intense collaboration with nature is evidenced in the monasteries and gardens of Japan. Lifetimes are spent in training in the craft and design of such spaces, through meditation and deep considerations for nature. All this to deliver an experiential moment of a lifetime, through an intimate encounter with the sensitivity and sensibility of these curated spaces and places.

Here in India, through thousands of years of building, great sensitivity has been demonstrated in the architecture of temples or in the less celebratory structures elsewhere in the landscape. There is an immense lesson to be learned from the unassuming architecture of villages and provincial towns of this country, where nature is omnipresent in shady courtyards, colorful streets or the informal village square spaced around that Banyan tree.

Often, the relationship between man and nature is emotional, just as it is in the delicate relationship between nature and architecture.

The advantage of nature

Man is in love with nature. Rare is one who has not been affected by the beauty of nature in one way or another. Beauty of nature. It is quite alarming how this word – beauty – has come to be nearly banished from our pages and our discourses. Discussions on aesthetics are almost always bombarded with a cocktail of complicated terminology and yet they fail to stir within us that feeling or emotion which this little word brings.

Have you ever seen an ugly landscape? Leave aside natural disasters and nature is unfailingly beautiful. The experience of this beauty sensitises us and our interaction with nature relieves us of the tension and stress of our increasingly hectic life.

Why else do we rush to these resorts that continue to appear in pristine settings? Disconnected from the rush of the city, we try to cleanse our system and rejuvenate, if it were possible. But stress is like a mould that leaves not easily in the few days of being in nature, only to set in deeper upon returning to fast-paced chaos.

And if this be the case, I propose that we turn our homes and work places into sanctuaries. I of course do not mean this literally but spatially – by way of the warmth and ambiance of the architecture and the atmosphere that the latter generates. If we cannot do this in our work places, then let us at least think of our homes and leisure spaces as treasury of calmness and serenity – where one may discover the advantages of solitude and silence. And it is in such a setting that nature can enter and prevail, and it is in deep communion with nature in this form of architecture that man can find himself – everyday and through his perils.

Many times it seems greenery is referred to as nature. It will pass without debate that vegetation, plants and forests present a lasting imagery of nature, but in constrained, expensive land parcels in the city, it may not always be possible to introduce greenery in a meaningful volume or manner. But decorative plants or planters are what they are: decoration. They neither express the beauty or spirit of nature nor provide the advantages of shade or coolness. However, there remain other elements of nature – sunlight, reflected light and half light; air, breeze, rain, water and fire. And if it is just one element, water let us say, it calls to be worked on to painful levels of detail and sensitivity. Perhaps there is no better example than that created by the master Swiss architect Peter Zumthor in his Therme Vals. Water, held in heavy containers of stone or softly caressed by light, becomes more precious than liquid gold.

Fountain in courtyard, Pavilion Apartment, Dhaka

And if it is just one tree that we have space for, then let it be the one which bears scented flowers or attracts birds. If it is only a patch of lawn we can afford, let it remain uncluttered so that children can know the joy of grass touching their bare feet. And when our buildings are out of the city and in wider landscapes, let us be tidy in our construction. Lest we confuse ourselves: the landscape is not for the building, but rather the building is subservient to the landscape.

The wonder of the interior

Is it not interesting to think that there is no "interior" in nature? Yes, there are the caves but caves are exteriors moving in or, if you will, exterior spaces without light. Even with the inclusion of caves, nature is essentially an "outdoor" phenomenon.

In a landscape, clouds are the roof of the great outdoor room, the rivers are its fountains, and rocks and trees its furniture. It is the drawing room of the Impressionists, a games room for the athletic and a study for the scientist. All of nature's beings live in this Great Outdoor Room.

But the intellect of man chose otherwise. Who knows what inspired the first builder to create that – now mythical – primordial hut? It was man's attempt to carve out a separate space for himself in the Great Outdoor Room. It was, in essence, a room within the grand room of nature and it held the seeds of man's first interior space.

If the primordial hut multiplied, it was because it appealed as a shelter to many. And from functional needs came the first wall, the first window and so on. The pavilion form became the first interiorised space. And then something magical happened: with the first enclosed space came the first created shadow, the first darkened corner. How restful that corner must have seemed. It became a place to sleep or for the ill to heal. In this way, the spaces chose their function and man responded with his use.

Today these first inspirations still exist: the pavilion form is for leisure and it embraces nature most freely. The darkest of all spaces is the bedroom – where the shadow induces sleep and the first light rushes through the window to usher in a new day. The spirit of the interior space has remained unchanged.

But every wall which bound the interior had an exterior surface – its face to nature – and this needed protection. Thus eaves were born and windows called for shading. And in man's unceasing urge to express, he looked at his hut no longer as a mere shelter but as an object in the Great Outdoor Room. Thus began the first study in form and expression – an occupation that will chase man till his last days on earth.

The house is the singular important event in the history of architecture. The design of a house could be the most inspiring commission for an architect. For the house is like a cosmos – it bears all the complexities of human life and yet keeps the seeds to man's inspirations.

The house is to a family, as much as the family is to a child. And the child holds the secrets to man's next inventions and to all of humanity's progress. Therefore, the house is easily the most important asset to a child and, by extension, to our various futures.

The house is a family of rooms. Like a family, the various rooms come together around the hearth – the living room – or the dinner table that is the dining room. Or it could be around a courtyard in which is a tree or a well. In this way the house is a close-knit weave of rooms. It has been so through millennia in our villages, in our culture. But now the house, as we know it, is changing.

With shifting lifestyles comes a wealth of rooms. Around the hearth are no longer gathered only the family rooms but they have been joined by a host of others. The house accommodates all, except that in a sprawling interior, the bonding – physical and emotional – seems to forever recede.

It is our experience that in architecture, more is not necessarily more. The interiors of the biggest projects are not necessarily the grandest, nor do they compulsorily embrace public life to the fullest. As in our houses, so too in our museums and in our spaces of commerce must we strike the right balance of scale and space, monumentality and intimacy. But the interior is, to a great extent, a function of culture – a subject I shall return to later.

The interiors of architecture require the greatest care by an architect. It is where one may touch a door knob, walk barefoot, or simply be carried away in thought. The eye searches for details to hold onto, even if for a fleeting moment, and tactile and olfactory senses are active.

Viewing nature from the comfort of the interior is the luxury of the kings. In our palaces and forts, examples abound. In our new building we have the advantage of glass. A fascinating material, if there ever was one. So thin yet it affords so much, all the while remaining invisible. Large panels bring nature right into our interiors. We remain protected but we can be at one with nature. Or so it would seem.

With glass came air-conditioning and we were forever separated from the breeze, the smell of the first monsoon rain or the song of birds, known and unknown. We continued to love nature – but from a distance. And the distance was allowed to grow.

When was the last time you walked barefoot on grass? Or felt the rain on your face? But this separation is not our device, it is borrowed. It is the example of colder lands and yet we adopt it like it were ours. The time is ripe with the need for a reversal.

Let us open our interiors to the outside, let our architecture be at one with nature again. Let not the outside stop where the inside starts, let us invite it in. Let us fill our interiors with light and the rarer breeze, let us fill it with the scents of our flowers. Let us not merely see the rain but hear it and let us not merely hear it, let us sometimes soak in it. Let us hold on to the treasures of the shadow and that old, darkened corner.

And when we bring in light, let it become our light. When we propose rooms, let it be our kind of rooms. And when we create spaces for our citizens, let it have a flavour that is only ours and let it resonate to the pulse of our culture.

The joy of culture

Plagued is a people whose culture is shallow.

Here in India it is difficult to imagine life without culture. From birth, marriage and death, from our seasons and celebrations to our attitudes, culture governs Indian life and living. So much that the common Indian may not be able to distinctly separate cultural components from everyday life – such is the intertwining.

But this indeed is a special occasion. I may not be able to proclaim the same in many other societies for the strength of culture is not universal throughout the world.

In comparatively newer settlements, like in the United States, the amalgamation of various cultures have resulted in yet newer cultures. But for us, culture is, it would seem, as old as the moon and it has settled deep into the veins of social life in more ways than we are aware.

Consequently it is quite impossible to ignore the impact of culture on our art. But in architecture, the function of culture is a complex one – one that is difficult to subscribe to and it may be misleading to ascribe physical attributes of architecture to culture, even in traces.

What is more easily apprehensible to the architect, however, is the culture of building. India has hundreds, if not thousands, of years of heritage of building. From earthen huts to high citadels of stone, we have gathered the knowledge and the wisdom of building in a most varied way.

And to draw inspiration from this rich tapestry of culture of building is to draw water from the deepest glaciers – old yet the freshest of waters. Here we must exercise extreme caution in drawing clues from our culture of building, lest we should fall into the vagaries of kitsch. The vernacular is for the vernacular, it is not for the contemporary – to copy from it is to draw its life breath out. The inspired architect must include and exclude, choose and distill, for the new architecture to be infused with the golden dust of history and the spirit of the vernacular, represents a singularly exciting event.

Throughout the world we have wonderful examples of works of architecture having drawn inspiration from the culture of building of that place. This not only gives inner strength in line with the proposals by Frampton in his "Critical Regionalism" but also does away with the flatness of a so-called "contemporary" style, having been born nowhere in particular but spreading everywhere. And there is no surer example of this than in the works of one of the greatest architects of our time, that of Álvaro Siza Vieira in Portugal.

The plain, whitewashed surfaces of the Portuguese wall in the villages has been taken to transcendent levels by Siza. The mundane becomes the celebrated and in his hands, the vernacular transforms the contemporary.

But this massive shift in architecture in Portugal cannot be attributed to Siza alone. He learned from Fernando Tavora and mentored Souto de Moura, the latter himself becoming a veritable force in the Portuguese scene. And is it not interesting to note that these three architects from generations separate, held offices on the three floors of the same building? Such is their cohesion, such is their revolution.

In India, if there is to be a revolution in architectural culture, it must be sponsored by strong forces, supported by others with similarly strong resolve. Separated, unrelated efforts will not bring true impetus for change.

Society of buildings

Society is a function of the many. Here the will of the individual is superseded by the need that is adjudged common.

Society is greater than the sum of its collective citizenry. Society is for all who come together to form it and does not necessarily pay exclusive attention to the individual. But architects are individuals and architecture, in many instances, belongs to individual authorship.

And in creating architecture for society, all architects are not equal – in talent, inspiration or focus of intentions. Therefore all buildings erected for the common do not necessarily reflect, to good extent, the culture or aspirations of that society. In fact, sadly, the reality is quite to the contrary.

Everywhere much of our civic architecture is devoid of the capacity to inspire its citizens. Many times, they are mute at best, alien at their worst.

And so society must be willing to go to great pains to select and nominate its architects for its civic facilities and must be exceedingly critical in accepting new architecture in the public realm.

The city is the physical manifestation of a society growing large. Cities are born when people come together to avail the benefits of its institutions, facilities and culture. They come to trade, to learn, to invent and to fall in love. Cities represent the greatest energy of man's aspirations and they hold the archive of our collective memory. Cities are the fruits of civilisation and they are the spearhead of man's future histories.

Cities exist because architecture exists. Without the manifestation of architecture, there can be no city.

The physical map of the city is a society of buildings. In between buildings are the streets and in between streets are the parks. A city decries its sprawl, in the same way as its citizens decry the loss of its open spaces.

The greatest assets of a city are not its buildings but its public spaces. The only way buildings can stay healthy in a city is to make way for the generosity of its public spaces.

Public spaces are the lungs of the body politic.

Public spaces are a function of the culture of that society. It reflects the nature of its people and speaks of their future. That is why the people like to gather in those spaces, to see and be seen, to hear and be heard.

Therefore the society invests in the architect great responsibility for the design of its public spaces.

Many times we look at public spaces and greens as negative to the positive – that is, if the buildings were masses – positive – then the spaces in the city would be its empty masses – negative. But let us call for a reversal to this. Let us generate the design of our cities from public spaces and let us fill the gaps in between with buildings and facilities. In this way we can be sure of our priorities – that in a city, architecture is answerable to its public spaces and the public spaces are answerable to its citizenry.

Why do we make strong distinctions between urban design and architecture? They are one and the same. The rooms become the building, buildings come together to define spaces and parks, and mark out the streets in a city. Of course, it is much more complex, and planning data and surveys will assist the architect in his design. The architect is the master of the form and its spaces and how these effect and affect cultures. Bring back the architect to design your cities and you will see the cities of your future.

Spirit, spirituality

Spirituality is in the essence of man. I refer not only to the spirituality of man's life on earth or to man's beliefs, but more to the spirituality of the land and its culture. Charged with spirituality is the land of India.

Yoga is an act of spirituality.

What is it about the Himalayas that overcame man to embrace Yoga? The spirit of the Himalayas is in Yoga but we do not necessarily need to be in the Himalayas to practice it. Nor does Yoga belong to the Indian – it has been given to the world.

But one who approaches Yoga as a physical act alone will never know its true essence. It is a communiqué to the soul as much as it is to the mind.

The Yogi still yearns to return to the Himalayas.

The Ganga is not a river, Ganga is a spirit. She does not belong to the world, she belongs to those who worship her. And to the lands through which she passes.

Rajasthan is not a province. It is the spirit of the desert given shape by man's culture. The architecture of Rajasthan is impregnated with the spirituality of the land.

In Rome, the Pantheon is timeless. Not so because of the decoration, ornamentation or any one element of architecture. It is the resultant spirit that is timeless. The oculus in the dome harkens back to the first time man raised his gaze to the zenith and wondered about the skies, his existence, his mortality. It is the surest dome in architecture – all others are derivatives from it and the influence is forever.

The spirit of the Pantheon is eternal.

A very similar spirit is embedded in our architecture of old. The Kailash temple in Ellora is eternal. Man did not make it, it was discovered by cutting into the earth and removing all that was not necessary – to reveal its forms and shadows to the sun. It is the epitome of the eternal spirit of architecture in India.

I will not dwell on this further but will wish that in a similar manner, the architecture we create is also touched by the spirit of eternity.

Architects embark not on a mission but on a journey –
a journey of learning and experiences – which proposes to
the architect his various creative productions. And due to
his culture, his inspiration, the architect distills his thought
and work before it is brought to greater light. An architect learns more than he can ever make and today I have
shared with you some of my learning.

Architecture is built of anything but words.

Photography credits

All photographs by Kashef Chowdhury except:
Cover photo: Hélène Binet, Ruins in Agarpur, Barisal
Page 25: Hélène Binet, Friendship Centre, Gaibandha
Page 31: Hélène Binet, Friendship Hospital, Satkhira
Page 33: Hélène Binet, Monk's cell, Vasu Vihar Monastery, Bogra, 7th–8th century AD
Page 49: Niklaus Graber, Art Gallery, Srihatta – Samdani Art Foundation, Sylhet
Page 51: Asif Salman, University of Liberal Arts, Dhaka
Page 55: Hélène Binet, Friendship Centre, Gaibandha
Page 59: Asif Salman, Satellite clinic, Remote location, Mongla
Page 61: Hélène Binet, Reception Pavilion, Friendship Centre, Gaibandha
Page 63: Hélène Binet, Concrete Mosque, Chittagong
Page 67: Limon Khan, House in Agarpur, Barisal
Page 73: Hélène Binet, Cast iron screen, Concrete Mosque, Chittagong
Page 75: Eric Chenal, Glass Labyrinth, Venice
Page 77: Hélène Binet, Pavilion, Abahani Sports Club, Dhaka
Page 81: Hélène Binet, Red Mosque, Keraniganj
Page 89: Niklaus Graber, Álvaro Siza Vieira, Boa Nova Tea House, Matosinhos
Page 99: Shakil Ibne Hai, Independence Monument, Dhaka
Page 101: Hélène Binet, Friendship Hospital, Satkhira
Page 115: Hélène Binet, Cyclone Shelter, Kuakata

Projects by Kashef Chowdhury / URBANA except Pavilion Apartment,
Independence Monument and Museum by Kashef Chowdhury and
Marina Tabassum – URBANA.

Acknowledgements

Kashef Chowdhury is grateful to the late Mobashsher Hossain for insisting on the
lecture at the Commonwealth conference.
He also thanks Shirish Beri for his invitation and persistence to deliver the
keynote at the Kolhapur conference.
Thanks to Niklaus for his unremitting support. Thanks to Linus for his openness
and to Ladina and Beat for this wonderful design.

Imprint

This publication is made possible by the generous support
of Marc Elvinger.

Author: Kashef Chowdhury
Publication project: Quart Verlag Luzern – Linus Wirz
Copy editing: Benjamin Liebelt, Berlin
Lithography: Printeria, Lucerne
Lithography, cover: Georg Sidler, Schwyz
Graphic design: BKVK, Basel – Ladina Ingold, Beat Keusch
Font: Happy Times by Lucas Le Bihan (Velvetyne Type foundry)
Paper: Kamiko Fly, 120g/m²
Printing and binding: DZA Druckerei zu Altenburg GmbH

This book is also published in German / Ebenfalls publiziert
in Deutsch (ISBN 978-3-03761-302-3)

Quart Publishers is being supported by the Federal Office of Culture
for the years 2021–2024.

Quart Verlag GmbH
Denkmalstrasse 2, CH-6006 Luzern
books@quart.ch, www.quart.ch